Qui...
nox horrifica

a *scary* Latin Novella
by Lance Piantaggini

Poētulus Publishing
magisterp.com

Index Capitulōrum
(et Cētera)

Praefātiō

Pīsō Ille Poētulus was the first Latin novella in the collection that has become known as the "Pisoverse." *Pīsō* was published in November of 2016, written with 108 unique words (excluding names, different forms of words, and meaning established within the text). Since then, new characters have been introduced in other novellas ranging from 20 to 104 unique words. Quintus has appeared briefly in *Rūfus et gladiātōrēs: Student FVR Reader*, as well as *Drūsilla et convīvium magārum.* Quintus now has his own story in this latest novella of 52 unique words (*excluding different forms of the same word, names, and meaning established within the text*), and is a quick read at over 1100 total words in length.

Although a low unique word count isn't everything, it's certainly most things when it comes to the beginning student reading Latin. Most available texts, however, are written with far too many words to be read with ease. *Quīntus et nox horrifica* is the latest novella to address this lack of understandable reading material with sheltered (i.e. limited) vocabulary available to beginning Latin students.

Like other recent novellas, *Quīntus* was written with many "super clear cognates" generated from a shared document (*search on magisterp.com*), accounting for half (26) of the 52 unique words! With the low unique word counts, and numerous cognates, the Pisoverse novellas now provide over 31,000 total words for the beginning Latin student to read! That's with a vocabulary of just 410 unique words across all current novellas (12)!

Quīntus et nox horrifica was inspired by those perfunctory "Roman House Units" included in the textbooks of yore. What better way to become familiar with the layout of the Roman house than a scary novella? *Quīntus* would also be a quick read for anyone interested in Pliny's ghost story.

The *Index Verbōrum* is rather comprehensive, with an English equivalent and example phrases from the text found under each vocabulary word. Meaning is established for every single word form in this novella.

I'd like to thank Bob Patrick and John Piazza for those intriguing conversations regarding grammar curiosities. I'd also like to thank my wife—whose Latin is improving so much that I soon need to find new barometer learner—for reading through this story, despite it being scary. Just like in *Rūfus et Lūcia: līberī lutulentī*, I have tried my hand at a bit of drawing, but lastly, and chiefly, the illustrations by Lauren Aczon provide significant comprehension support for the novice reading *Quīntus*. See more of Lauren's artwork on Instagram @leaczon, and/or on her blog, (www.quickeningforce.blogspot.com).

Magister P[iantaggini]
Northampton, MA
September 16th, 2018

prologus

mōnstra et phantasmata[1]...

...sintne realia?![2]

---

[1] **mōnstra et phantasmata** *monsters and phantasms (i.e. ghosts)*
[2] **sintne realia?** *Could they be real?!*

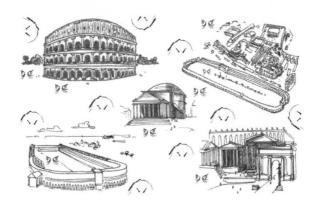

Rōmae, erant mōnstra varia!

Rōmae, erant phantasmata violenta!

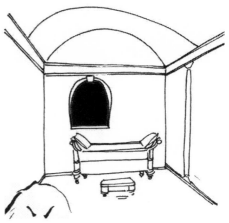

Rōmānī habēbant mōnstra et phantasmata, domī.[3]

---

[3] **domī** *at home*

haBĒSne[4] mōnstra et phantasmata, domī?

vīDISTĪne[5] mōnstrum?

vīDISTĪne phantasmatem?

sunt mōnstra et phantasmata, ubīque —horrōrem![6]

---

[4] **haBĒSne?** *Do YOU have?*
[5] **vīDISTĪne?** *Have YOU seen?*
[6] **horrōrem!** *What horror!*

I
parentēs domī nōn sunt

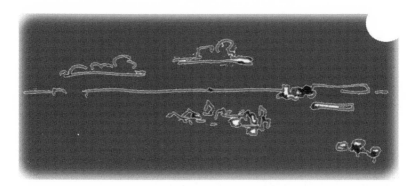

est nox.

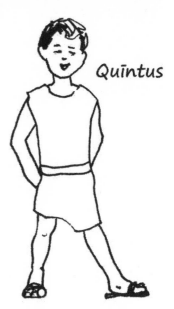

Quīntus

Quīntus domī est.

subitō, Quīntus
aliquid audit.

Quīntus parentēs nōn audit.
parentēs Quīntī nōn sunt domī.

Quīntus sonum horrificum audit.
Quīntus putat aliquid esse[1] domī.

Quīntus iterum audit sonum
horrificum.

Quīntus:
"sitne mōnstrum?![2]
sitne phantasma?!"

Quīntus sonum investīgat...

---

[1] **putat aliquid esse** *thinks that something is*
[2] **sitne mōnstrum?!** *Could it be a monster?!*

II
sonum investīgāns

Quīntus sonum audīvit.
sonus horrificus fuit.[1]

Quīntus est Rōmānus cūriōsus, sed cautus. Quīntus nōn vult vidēre mōnstrum! Quīntus nōn vult vidēre phantasmatem!

sed, Quīntus sonum investīgāre vult.

cautē, Quīntus sonum investīgat...

---

[1] **fuit** *was*

Quīntus putat sonum esse ab ātriō.[2]

ātrium

Quīntus ātrium investīgat,
sed cautē investīgat.

ātrium īnspectum est ā Quīntō. sed, in ātriō nōn est mōnstrum. in ātriō, Quīntus phantasmatem nōn videt.

in ātriō est silentium.
ātrium tranquillum est.

---

[2] **ab ātriō** *from the atrium (i.e. large room with open roof)*

Quīntus:
"estne sonus realis?"

Quīntus rīdet. Quīntus
putat sonum nōn esse
realem.

tranquillus, Quīntus iam vult dormīre.

Quīntus vult dormīre in cubiculō. sed,
Quīntus vult iānuam esse³ apertam.

---

³ **vult iānuam esse** *wants the door to be*

Quīntus iānuam cubiculī nōn claudit. in cubiculō, Quīntus iam dormītūrus est.[4]

subitō, Quīntus sonum iterum audit!

Quīntus:
"sonus EST realis!"

sonus est horrificus — nōn — HORRIFICISSIMUS!

sonus murmur est. Quīntus murmur audit. sed, sonus nōn est ab ātriō. est murmur horrificissimum, domī!

Quīntus:
"murmur nōn est nātūrāle! murmur horrificissimum est! aliquid EST domī! sitne mōnstrum?! sitne phantasma?!"

---

[4] **dormītūrus est** *is about to sleep*

iam, Quīntus est perterritus![5]

Quīntus iānuam cubiculī claudit!

Quīntus, perterritus,
vult parentēs esse domī...

III
affectus est murmure

Quīntus dormīre voluit. sed, fuit sonus horrificissimus domī. sonus nātūrālis nōn fuit! sonus fuit murmur horrificissimum. horrōrem!

Quīntus murmur iterum audit.

Quīntus est affectus murmure.[1]

---

[1] **est affectus murmure** *is affected by the murmur*

Quīntus investīgāre sonum nōn vult. Quīntus tranquillus nōn est. Quīntus est perterritus et immobilis!

sonus nōn est ab ātriō. Quīntus iam putat murmur esse ā culīnā.

culīna

Quīntus iānuam cubiculī aperit.

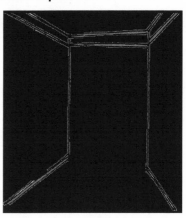

<creeeeeeek>

nox est. ā cubiculō,[2] Quīntus nōn videt culīnam.

---

[2] **ā cubiculō** *from the bedroom [view]*

Quīntus oculōs claudit.
Quīntus nōn vult vidēre
mōnstrum.

Quīntus phantasmatem
vidēre nōn vult.

oculīs clausīs,[3] Quīntus audit...

subitō, Quīntus audit sonōs variōs
ubīque domī!

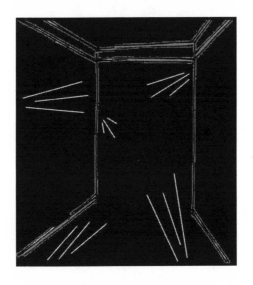

sonī variī nōn sunt mortālēs!
sonī variī nōn sunt nātūrālēs!

---

[3] **oculīs clausīs** *with eyes now closed*

Quīntus iterum claudit iānuam cubiculī!

Quīntus:
"sunt sonī mōnstrōrum
et phantasmatum!
habeō mōnstra, domī!
habeō phantasmata, domī!"

subitō—silentium.

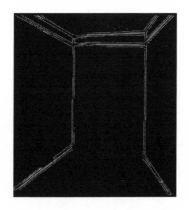

est silentium ubīque domī.

Quīntus:
"erant sonī variī et horrificī
ubīque domī. iam, silentium?!
iam, domus tranquilla est?!"

Quīntus, perterritus sed cūriōsus, cautē aperit iānuam.

subitō, Quīntus aliquid videt...

Quīntus figūram videt!!!!

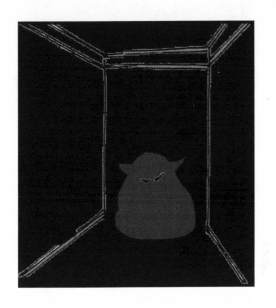

nocte, figūra obscūra est. sed, figūra nātūrālis nōn est. figūra est... MŌNSTRUM—horrōrem!

* * *

subitō, Quīntus surgit.

nōn sunt sonī. nōn sunt murmura.
iānua cubiculī clausa est.

Quīntus:
"dormiēbam![4] sonī
realēs nōn erant."

Quīntus rīdet.

Quīntus tranquillē aperit
iānuam cubiculī.

_____

[4] **dormiēbam** *I was sleeping*

22

Quīntus nōn videt figūram obscūram.
Quīntus mōnstrum nōn videt.

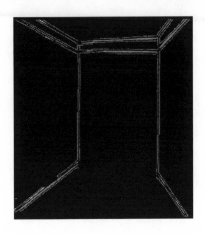

Quīntus tranquillē rīdet.

Quīntus:
"putābam mōnstrum
esse[5] domī."

Quīntus iterum rīdet.

sed...

IV
iterum?!

subitō, Quīntus aliquid audit!

Quīntus:
"iterum?!"

iānuā apertā,[1] Quīntus sonum
metallicum et clārum audit.
sed, sonus metallicus nōn est horrificus.

Quīntus perterritus nōn est.

---

[1] **iānuā apertā** *since the door has been opened*

Quīntus putat sonum esse ā peristȳlō.[2]

peristȳlum

Quīntus cūriōsus est. Quīntus
peristȳlum cūriōsē investīgat...

nox est. peristȳlum est obscūrum.

---

[2] **ā peristȳlō** *from the peristyle, a covered walkway*
outside with a garden

peristӯlum cautē īnspectum est ā Quīntō. sed, in peristӯlō nōn est phantasma. in peristӯlō, Quīntus mōnstrum nōn videt.

est silentium in peristӯlō.
peristӯlum est tranquillum.

subitō, Quīntus audit aliquid ā triclīniō!³

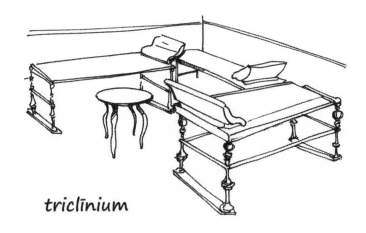

triclīnium

Quīntus:
"ITERUM?!"

---

³ **ā triclīniō** *from the dining room*

Quīntus iam perturbātus est!

Quīntus triclīnium investīgat...

V
aliquid sentiēns

Quīntus sonum iterum audīvit.
Quīntus iam nōn est cautus.
Quīntus perturbātus est.

Quīntus:
"est sonus, iterum?!
dormītūrus fuī,[1] sed
audīvī sonōs variōs.
erat silentium domī.
iam, iterum sunt sonī?!"

Quīntus, perturbātus,
triclīnium investīgat.

---

[1] **dormītūrus fuī** *I was about to fall asleep*

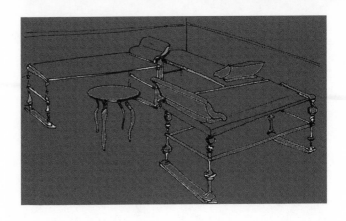

in triclīniō obscūrō, Quīntus videt aliquid. sed, Quīntus nōn videt clārē, nocte.

Quīntus:
"attat!"[2]

sed, Quīntus videt
mēnsam, nōn mōnstrum.

in triclīniō obscūrō, Quīntus iterum videt aliquid. sed, nox est. nocte, Quīntus nōn videt clārē.

---

[2] **attat!** *Ah ha!*

Quīntus:
"attat!"

sed, Quīntus videt lectum,
nōn phantasmatem.

Quīntus, perturbātus:
"sonī realēs nōn sunt!
estne nox perpetua?!?!
volōōōō dorrrrmīīīīīīīre!"

subitō, Quīntus aliquid sentit[3]...

---

[3] **aliquid sentit** *senses something*

Quīntus sentit aliquid nōn nātūrāle.
Quīntus sentit aliquid nōn mortāle.
Quīntus sentit...phantasmatem!

horrōrem!

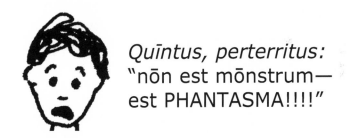

Quīntus, perterritus:
"nōn est mōnstrum—
est PHANTASMA!!!!"

Quīntus immobilis est.

subitō, mēnsa surgit!

Quīntus ferē cacat.[4]

---

[4] **ferē cacat** *almost poops*

subitō, lectī surgunt!

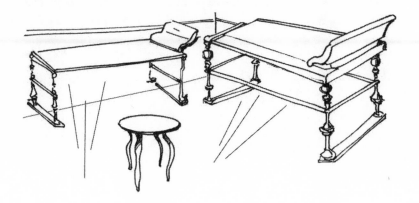

Quīntus est cōram phantasmate.[5]

stomachus Quīntī turbulentus est.
Quīntus nauseam habet.

---

[5] **cōram phantasmate** *in the presence of a ghost*

mēnsā et lectīs surrectīs,[6] Quīntus putat phantasmatem esse violentum! Quīntus nōn vult phantasmatem, domī. sed, Quīntus clārē nōn vult phantasmatem *violentum*, domī!

subitō, iānuae ubīque domī aperiunt et claudunt!

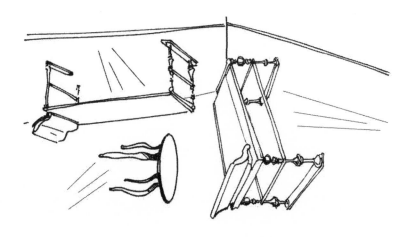

iam, triclīnium est turbulentissimum. domus turbulentissima est. Quīntus est perterritissimus!

---

[6] **mēnsā et lectīs surrectīs** *table and couches having been lifted up*

Quīntus nōn vult vidēre phantasmatem in triclīniō.

Quīntus oculōs claudit...

35

VI
ēvidentia phantasmatis

Quīntus oculōs aperit.

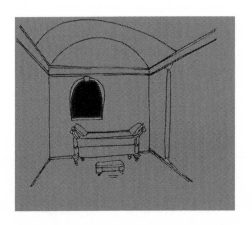

Quīntus in cubiculō iam est. iānua cubiculī aperta est. nōn sunt sonī horrificī. iterum, est silentium domī.

Quīntus:
"dormiēbam...ITERUM?!"

Quīntus nōn rīdet. Quīntus perturbātus iterum est.

Quīntus triclīnium investīgat, sed perturbātē investīgat.

Quīntus lectōs videt. lectī nōn surrectī sunt. Quīntus mēnsam videt. mēnsa nōn surrecta est.

nōn est ēvidentia phantasmatis.[1] Quīntus ēvidentiam turbulentiae nōn videt. Quīntus nōn videt ēvidentiam violentiae.

---

[1] **ēvidentia phantasmatis** *evidence of a ghost*

Quīntus vult esse in cubiculō. Quīntus dormīre vult. sed, Quīntus putat noctem esse[2] perpetuam. Quīntus iam īnsomniam habet!

sonī nōn erant reālēs.
nōn erant mōnstra in ātriō.

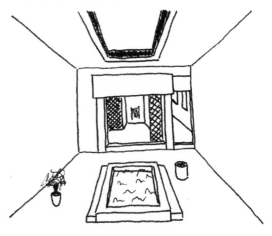

nōn erant phantasmata in culīnā.

---

[2] **putat noctem esse** *thinks that the night is*

in peristȳlō et in triclīniō nōn erant mōnstra...

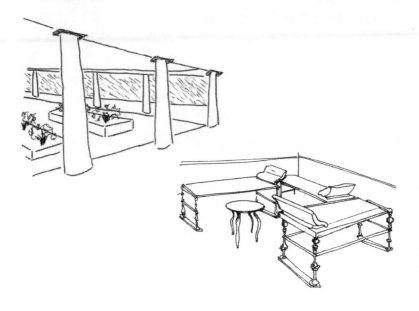

..et ubīque domī
phantasmata nōn erant!

Quīntus, perturbātus:
"ferē cacāvī. sed, sonī nōn
realēs erant! iam, dormīre
volō. sed, īnsomniam
habeō. perturbātus sum!"

subitō, Quīntus iterum audit
sonōs metallicōs.

Quīntus:
"iterum?! I—TE—RUM?!?!"

Quīntus audit sonōs metallicōs
ā tablīnō.[3]

tablīnum

Quīntus, perturbātissimus, investīgat
sonōs metallicōs in tablīnō...

---

[3] **ā tablīnō** *from the office/study*

VII
armārium īnspiciēns

Quīntus tablīnum investīgat, perturbātē. sed, in tablīnō est silentium. Quīntus sonōs nōn audit.

tablīnō obscūrō nocte,[1] Quīntus clārē nōn videt. sed, Quīntus aliquid in tablīnō videt. nōn est phantasma.

---

[1] **tablīnō obscūrō nocte** *with the study obscured by night*

est...armārium.[2]

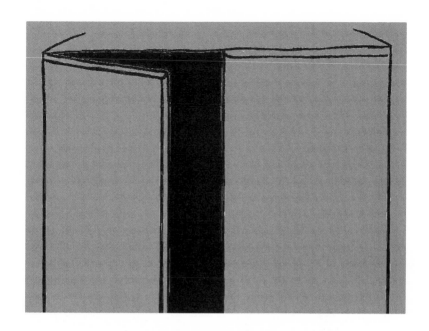

armārium clausum nōn est.
armārium apertum est.

Quīntus putāvit armārium fuisse[3]
clausum.

sed, iam armārium apertum est.

---

[2] **armārium** *armoire (i.e. moveable clothing closet)*
[3] **putāvit armārium fuisse** *thought that the closet had been*

Quīntus:
"armārium apertum est?!
est cūriōsum."[4]

Quīntus armārium īnspicere vult.
Quīntus armārium īnspicit, sed cautē.

subitō, Quīntus videt oculōs in armāriō!

Quīntus immobilis est.
oculī nātūrālēs nōn sunt.
oculī mortālēs nōn sunt.

---

[4] **est cūriōsum** *it's a curious thing*

nōn est phantasma...est MŌNSTRUM!

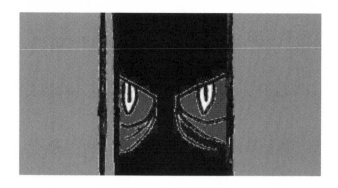

mōnstrum habet oculōs obscūrōs
et horrificōs!

Quīntus, perterritus, ferē cacat.

Quīntus:
"mōnstrum est reale!
nōn dormiō! est mōnstrum
horrificum in armāriō!"

stomachus Quīntī iterum
est turbulentus.

Quīntus nauseam iterum habet.

subitō, Quīntus sentit
aliquid cūriōsum...

Quīntus nōn est cōram mōnstrō.

Quīntus est cōram...

VIII
cōram...

Quīntus est cōram...
Lūciā, et Drūsillā, et Sextō!?!?!

Lūcia

Drūsilla

Sextus

Lūcia, Drūsilla, et Sextus
fefellērunt[1] Quīntum!

Quīntus:
"mē fefellistis—macte!"[2]

Lūcia, Drūsilla, Sextus, et Quīntus
rīdent.

Lūcia:
"Quīnte, cacāvistī?"

Quīntus:
"ferē!"

Lūcia rīdet.

---

[1] **fefellērunt** *tricked*
[2] **mē fefellistis—macte!** *You all tricked me—well done!*

Quīntus:
"mōnstrum reale nōn erat?"

Drūsilla:
"erat mōnstrum
falsum!"

Drūsilla mōnstrum falsum habet.

Quīntus:
"attat! et oculī
realēs nōn erant?"

Sextus:
"oculī erant falsī!"

Sextus oculōs falsōs habet!

Quīntus:
"attat! sed, sonōs audīvī.
sonī falsī nōn erant
—erantne?"

Lūcia:
"sonī realēs erant."

Lūcia metallica[3] habet.

Quīntus:
"attat! erant sonī horrificī ubīque. eram perterritus! mēnsa et lectī surrectī sunt —macte!"

---

[3] **metallica** *metallic things*

subitō, Lūcia, Drūsilla, et Sextus
iam nōn rīdent.

Lūcia:
"sed, Quīnte..."

Quīntus:
"iānuae aperuērunt et
clausērunt ubīque—macte!"

Lūcia, Drūsilla, et Sextus iam sunt
immobilēs, et perterritī, et ferē cacant!

Drūsilla:
"Quīnte, nōn erāmus..."

Quīntus:
"et phantasm—"

Sextus:
"—Quīnte, audī!"

Quīntus iam nōn rīdet.

Lūcia, Drūsilla, et Sextus:
"nōn...nōn erāmus in triclīniō..."

nox est. domus obscūra est.

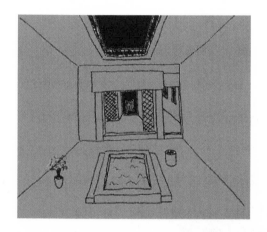

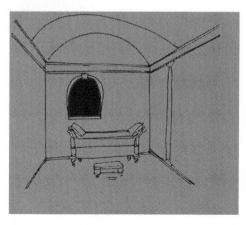

subitō...

Index Verbōrum

A

ā/ab *from, away from, by*
affectus *affected*
    affectus murmure *affected by the murmur*
aliquid *something*
    aliquid audit *hears something*
    putat aliquid esse *thinks that something is*
    aliquid videt *sees something*
    aliquid sentīre *to sense something*
aperit *opens*
    iānuam aperit *opens the door*
    cautē aperit *cautiously opens*
    tranquillē aperit *calmly opens*
    oculōs aperit *opens eyes*
  aperiunt *(more than one) open*
    iānuae aperiunt *doors open*
  aperta *open*
    iānua aperta *an open door*
  apertā *has been opened*
    iānuā apertā *since the door has been opened*
  apertam *open*
    vult iānuam esse apertam *wants the door to be open*
  apertum *open*
    armārium apertum *an open closet*
  aperuērunt *(more than one) opened*
    iānuae aperuērunt *doors opened*
armāriō *armoire (i.e. moveable clothing closet)*
    in armāriō *in the closet*
  armārium *armoire*
    armārium īnspicere *to inspect the closet*
ātriō *atrium, large room with open roof*
    ab ātriō *from the atrium*
    in ātriō *in the atrium*
  ātrium *atrium*
    ātrium investīgat *investigates the atrium*
    ātrium īnspectum est *atrium has been inspected*
attat! *Ah ha!*
audit *hears, listens*
    aliquid audit *hears something*
    parentēs nōn audit *doesn't hear parents*
    sonum audit *hears a sound*
    murmur audit *hears a murmur*

Quīntus audit *Quintus listens*
   sonōs variōs audit *hears various sounds*
audīvī *I heard*
   sonōs audīvī *I heard sounds*
audīvit *heard*
   sonum audīvit *heard a sound*

C

cacant *(more than one) kaka, poop*
   ferē cacant *almost poop*
  cacat *poops*
   ferē cacat *almost poops*
  cacāvī *I pooped*
   ferē cacāvī *I almost pooped*
  cacāvistī *you pooped*
cautē *cautiously*
  cautus *cautious*
   Rōmānus cautus *cautious Roman*
clārē *clearly*
  clārum *clear*
   sonum clārum *clear sound*
claudit *closes, shuts*
   iānuam claudit *shuts the door*
   oculōs claudit *closes eyes*
  claudunt *(more than one) are shut*
   iānuae claudunt *doors are shut*
  clausa *closed*
   iānua clausa *a closed door*
  clausērunt *(more than one) shut*
   iānuae clausērunt *doors shut*
  clausīs *have been closed*
   oculīs clausīs *with eyes now closed*
  clausum *closed*
   armārium clausum *a closed closet*
cōram *in the presence of*
   cōram phantasmate *in the presence of a ghost*
   cōram mōnstrō *in the presence of a monster*
cubiculī *of the room, bedroom*
   iānuam cubiculī *door of the bedroom*
  cubiculō *room, bedroom*
   in cubiculō *in the bedroom*
   ā cubiculō *from the bedroom [view]*
culīnā *kitchen*
   ā culīnā *from the kitchen*

culīnam *kitchen*
    nōn videt culīnam *doesn't see the kitchen*
cūriōsum *curious*
    est cūriōsum *it's a curious thing*
    aliquid cūriōsum *something curious*
  cūriōsus *curious*
    Rōmānus cūriōsus *curious Roman*

D, E, F, H
domī *at home*
  domus *house*
    domus tranquilla *calm house*
dormiēbam *I was sleeping*
  dormiō *I sleep*
    nōn dormiō! *I'm not sleeping!*
  dormīre *to sleep*
    velle dormīre *to want to sleep*
  dormītūrus est *about to sleep*
  dormītūrus fuī *I was about to sleep*
eram *I was*
  erāmus *we were*
  erant *(more than one) were, there were*
  erantne? *Were they?*
  erat *was*
  esse *to be*
  est *is, there is*
  estne? *Is?*
et *and*
ēvidentia *evidence*
  ēvidentiam *evidence*
    ēvidentiam nōn videt *doesn't see evidence*
ferē *almost*
figūra *a figure*
  figūram *a figure*
    figūram videt *sees a figure*
fuī *I was (briefly)*
  fuisse *to have been*
    putāvit armārium fuisse *thought that the closet had been*
  fuit *was*
habēbant *(more than one) had*
    habēbant mōnstra *had monsters*
    habēbant phantasmata *had ghosts*
  habeō *I have*
    habeō mōnstra *I have monsters*
    habeō phantasmata *I have ghosts*

īnsomniam habeō *I have insomnia*

haBĒSne? *Do YOU have?*

haBĒSne mōnstra? *Do YOU have monsters?*

haBĒSne phantasmata? *Do YOU have ghosts?*

habet *has*

nauseam habet *has nausea*

īnsomniam habet *has insomnia*

habet oculōs *has eyes*

horrificī *horrific (more than one)*

sonī horrificī *horrific sounds*

horrificissimum *really horrific*

murmur horrificissimum *really horrific murmur*

horrificissimus *really horrific*

sonus horrificissimus *really horrific sound*

horrificōs *horrific (more than one)*

oculōs horrificōs *horrific eyes*

horrificum *horrific*

sonum horrificum *horrific sound*

mōnstrum horrificum *horrific monster*

horrificus *horrific*

sonus horrificus *horrific sound*

horrōrem! *What horror!*

I

iam *now*

iānua *door*

iānuā *door*

iānuā apertā *since the door has been opened*

iānuae *doors*

iānuam *door*

vult iānuam esse apertam *wants the door to be open*

iānuam claudit *shuts the door*

iānuam aperit *opens the door*

immobilēs *immobile (more than one)*

immobilis *immobile*

Quīntus immobilis *immobile Quintus*

in *in*

īnsomniam *insomnia (i.e. can't sleep)*

īnsomniam habēre *to have insomnia*

īnspectum est *has been inspected*

īnspectum est ā Quīntō *inspected by Quintus*

īnspicere *to inspect*

armārium īnspicere *to inspect the closet*

īnspiciēns *inspecting*

armārium īnspiciēns *inspecting the closet*

īnspicit *inspects*
    armārium īnspicit *inspects the closet*
investīgāns *investigating*
    sonum investīgāns *investigating the sound*
    investīgāre *to investigate*
    sonum investīgāre *to investigate a sound*
    investīgat *investigates*
    sonum investīgat *investigates the sound*
    cautē investīgat *cautiously investigates*
    ātrium investīgat *investigates the atrium*
    cūriōsē investīgat *curiously investigates*
    peristȳlum investīgat *investigates the peristyle*
    triclīnium investīgat *investigates the dining room*
iterum *again*

L, M

lectī *couches*
    lectī surgunt *the couches rise*
    lectīs *couches*
    mēnsā et lectīs surrectīs *table and couches having been lifted up*

    lectōs *couches*
    lectōs videt *sees couches*
    lectum *couch*
    videt lectum *sees a couch*
macte! *Well done!*
mēnsa *table*
    mēnsa surgit *the table rises*
    mēnsā *table*
    mēnsā et lectīs surrectīs *table and couches having been lifted up*

    mēnsam *table*
    videt mēnsam *sees a table*
metallica *metallic (more than one)*
    metallica habet *has metallic things*
    metallicōs *metallic (more than one)*
    sonōs metallicōs *metallic sounds*
    metallicum *metallic*
    sonum metallicum *metallic sound*
mōnstra *monsters*
    habēre mōnstra *to have monsters*
    vidēre mōnstra *to see monsters*
    mōnstrō *monster*
    cōram mōnstrō *in the presence of a monster*

mōnstrōrum *of monsters*
    sonī mōnstrōrum *sounds of monsters*
mōnstrum *monster*
    sitne mōnstrum?! *Could it be a monster?!*
    vidēre mōnstrum *to see a monster*
    putābam mōnstrum esse *I thought that a monster was*
mortāle *mortal (i.e. can die)*
    aliquid nōn mortāle *something immortal*
  mortālēs *mortal (more than one)*
    sonī mortālēs *mortal sounds*
    oculī mortālēs *mortal eyes*
murmur *murmur (i.e. soft, indistinct, yet constant sound)*
    murmur audit *hears a murmur*
    putat murmur esse *thinks that the murmur is*
  murmure *murmur*
    affectus murmure *affected by the murmur*

N, O

nātūrāle *natural*
    murmur nōn est nātūrāle *the murmur isn't natural*
    aliquid nōn nātūrāle *something unnatural*
  nātūrālēs *natural (more than one)*
    sonī nātūrālēs *natural sounds*
    oculī nātūrālēs *natural eyes*
  nātūrālis *natural*
    sonus nātūrālis *natural sound*
    figūra nātūrālis *natural figure*
nauseam *nausea (i.e. sick feeling)*
    nauseam habet *has nausea*
nocte *at night*
  noctem *night*
    putat noctem esse *thinks that the night is*
nōn *not*
nox *night*
obscūra *obscured (i.e. dark)*
    figūra obscūra *dark figure*
  obscūram *dark*
    figūram obscūram *dark figure*
  obscūrō *dark*
    in triclīniō obscūrō *in the dark dining room*
    tablīnō obscūrō nocte *with the study obscured by night*
  obscūrōs *dark (more than one)*
    oculōs obscūrōs *dark eyes*
  obscūrum *dark*
    peristȳlum obscūrum *dark peristyle*

oculīs *eyes*
> oculīs clausīs *with eyes now closed*

oculōs *eyes*
> oculōs claudit *closes eyes*
> oculōs aperit *opens eyes*
> videt oculōs *sees eyes*
> oculōs realēs *real eyes*

P

parentēs *parents*
> parentēs nōn audit *doesn't hear parents*
> vult parentēs esse *wants parents to be*

peristȳlō *peristyle, covered walkway outside w/ garden*
> ā peristȳlō *from the peristyle*

peristȳlum *peristyle*
> peristȳlum investīgat *investigates the peristyle*

perpetua *perpetual (i.e. never-ending)*
> nox perpetua *perpetual night*

perpetuam *perpetual*
> noctem perpetuam *perpetual night*

perterritī *terrified (more than one)*
> **perterritissimus** *very terrified*
> Quīntus perterritissimus *very terrified Quintus*
> **perterritus** *terrified*
> Quīntus perterritus *terrified Quintus*

perturbātē *perturbedly (i.e. in an annoyed way)*
> **perturbātissimus** *very perturbed*
> Quīntus perturbātissimus *very perturbed Quintus*
> **perturbātus** *perturbed*
> Quīntus perturbātus *perturbed Quintus*

phantasmata *phantasms (i.e. ghosts)*
> habēre phantasmata *to have ghosts*
> vidēre phantasmata *to see ghosts*
> **phantasmate** *ghost*
> cōram phantasmate *in the presence of a ghost*
> **phantasmatem** *ghost*
> · vidēre phantasmatem *to see a ghost*
> sentit phantasmatem *senses a ghost*
> putat phantasmatem esse *thinks that the ghost is*
> nōn vult phantasmatem *doesn't want a ghost*
> **phantasmatis** *of a ghost*
> ēvidentia phantasmatis *evidence of a ghost*
> **phantasmatum** *of ghosts*
> sonī phantasmatum *sounds of ghosts*

putābam *I thought*
   putābam mōnstrum esse *I thought that a monster was*
   putat *thinks*
      putat aliquid esse *thinks that something is*
      putat sonum esse *thinks that the sound is*
      putat murmur esse *thinks that the murmur is*
      putat phantasmatem esse *thinks that the ghost is*
      putat noctem esse *thinks that the night is*
   putāvit *thought*
      putāvit armārium fuisse *thought that the closet had been*

Q, R, S

Quīntī *of Quintus, our terrified Roman, home alone*
      parentēs Quīntī *Quintus' parents*
      stomachus Quīntī *Quintus' stomach*
   Quīntō *Quintus*
      īnspectum est ā Quīntō *inspected by Quintus*
   Quīntus *Quintus*
      Quīntus audit *Quintus listens*
reale *real*
      mōnstrum reale *real monster*
   realem *real*
      sonum realem *real sound*
   realēs *real (more than one)*
      sonī realēs *real sounds*
   realia *real (more than one)*
      mōnstra et phantasmata realia *real monsters & ghosts*
   realis *real*
      sonus realis *real sound*
rīdent *(more than one) laugh*
   rīdet *laughs*
      tranquillē rīdet *laughs calmly*
Rōmae *in Rome*
Rōmānī *Romans*
   Rōmānus *Roman*
sed *but*
sentiēns *sensing*
      aliquid sentiēns *sensing something*
   sentit *senses*
      aliquid sentit *senses something*
      sentit phantasmatem *senses a ghost*
silentium *silence*
sintne? *Could they?*
      sintne realia? *Could they be real?*

sitne? *Could it be?*
    sitne mōnstrum?! *Could it be a monster?!*
    sitne phantasma?! *Could it be a ghost?!*
sonī *sounds*
  sonōs *sounds*
    sonōs variōs *various sounds*
  sonum *sound*
    sonum audīre *to hear a sound*
    sonum investīgāre *to investigate the sound*
    putat sonum esse *thinks that the sound is*
  sonus *sound*
stomachus *stomach*
subitō! *Suddenly!*
sunt *(more than one) are, there are*
surgit *gets up, rises*
    Quīntus surgit *Quintus gets up*
    mēnsa surgit *the table rises*
  surgunt *(more than one) rise*
    lectī surgunt *the couchs rise*
  surrecta est *was lifted up*
    mēnsa nōn surrecta est *the table wasn't lifted up*
  surrectī sunt *(more than one) were lifted up*
    lectī nōn surrectī sunt *the couches weren't lifted up*
  surrectīs *(more than one) lifted up*
    mēnsā et lectīs surrectīs *table and couches having been*
                               lifted up

T, U, V

tablīnō *the office/study room*
    ā tablīnō *from the study*
    in tablīnō *in the study*
    tablīnō obscūrō nocte *with the study obscured by night*
  tablīnum *study*
    tablīnum investīgat *investigates the study*
tranquilla *tranquil (i.e. calm)*
    domus tranquilla *calm house*
  tranquillē *calmly*
  tranquillum *calm*
    ātrium tranquillum *calm atrium*
    peristȳlum tranquillum *calm peristyle*
  tranquillus *calm*
    tranquillus Quīntus *calm Quintus*
triclīniō *the dining room*
    ā triclīniō *from the dining room*
  triclīnium *dining room*
    triclīnium investīgat *investigates the dining room*

turbulentiae *of turbulence (i.e. chaos)*
 ēvidentiam turbulentiae *evidence of turbulence*
turbulentissima *very turbulent (i.e. chaotic, upset)*
 domus turbulentissima *very turbulent house*
 turbulentissimum *very turbulent*
  triclīnium turbulentissimum *very turbulent dining room*
 turbulentus *turbulent, upset*
  stomachus turbulentus *upset stomach*
ubīque *everywhere*
varia *various*
 mōnstra varia *various monsters*
 variī *various*
  sonī variī *various sounds*
 variōs *various*
  sonōs variōs *various sounds*
vidēre *to see*
 vidēre mōnstrum *to see a monster*
 videt *sees*
  phantasmatem nōn videt *doesn't see a ghost*
  nōn videt culīnam *doesn't see the kitchen*
  aliquid videt *sees something*
  figūram videt *sees a figure*
  videt mēnsam *sees a table*
  videt lectum *sees a couch*
  ēvidentiam nōn videt *doesn't see evidence*
  videt oculōs *sees eyes*
 vīDISTĪne? *Have YOU seen?*
  vīDISTĪne mōnstrum? *Have YOU seen monster?*
  vīDISTĪne phantasmatem? *Have YOU seen a ghost?*
violenta *violent (more than one)*
 phantasmata violenta *violent ghosts*
 violentum *violent*
  phantasmatem violentum *violent ghost*
violentiae *violence*
 ēvidentiam violentiae *evidence of violence*
voluit *wanted*
 dormīre voluit *wanted to sleep*
vult *wants*
 nōn vult vidēre *doesn't want to see*
 investīgāre vult *wants to investigate*
 vult dormīre *wants to sleep*
 vult iānuam esse *wants the door to be*
 vult parentēs esse *wants parents to be*
 nōn vult phantasmatem *doesn't want a ghost*
 īnspicere vult *wants to inspect*

Pisoverse Novellas & Resources

Magister P's Pop-Up Grammar

Pop-Up Grammar occurs when a student—not teacher—asks about a particular language feature, and the teacher offers a very brief explanation in order to continue communicating (i.e. interpreting, negotiating, and expressing meaning during reading or interacting).

Teachers can use this resource to provide such explanations, or students can keep this resource handy for reference when the teacher is unavailable. Characters and details from the Pisoverse novellas are used as examples of the most common of common Latin grammar.

MAGISTER P's
POP-UP GRAMMAR
A 'QUICK' REFERENCE

Satisfying one's curiosity
about common features of Latin
in a comprehensible way

BY LANCE PIANTAGGINI

Level AA
Early Beginner

Mārcus magulus
(11 cognates + 8 other words)

Marcus likes being a young Roman mage, but such a conspicuous combo presents problems in Egypt after he and his parents relocate from Rome. Despite generously offering his magical talents, this young mage feels like an obvious outsider, sometimes wishing he were invisible. Have you ever felt that way? Marcus searches Egypt for a place to be openly accepted, and even has a run-in with the famously fiendish Sphinx! Can Marcus escape unscathed?

Olianna et obiectum magicum
(12 cognates + 12 other words)

Olianna is different from the rest of her family, and finds herself excluded as a result. Have you ever felt that way? One day, a magical object appears that just might change everything for good. However, will it really be for the better? Can you spot any morals in this tale told from different perspectives?

Rūfus lutulentus
(20 words)

Was there a time when you or your younger siblings went through some kind of gross phase? Rufus is a Roman boy who likes to be muddy. He wants to be covered in mud everywhere in Rome, but quickly learns from Romans who bathe daily that it's not OK to do so in public. Can Rufus find a way to be muddy?

Rūfus et Lūcia: līberī lutulentī
(25-70 words)

Lucia, of Arianne Belzer's Lūcia: puella mala, joins Rufus in this collection of 18 additional stories. This muddy duo has fun in the second of each chapter expansion. Use to provide more exposure to words from the novella, or as a Free Voluntary Reading (FVR) option for all students, independent from Rūfus lutulentus.

Quīntus et nox horrifica
(26 cognates, 26 other words)

Monsters and ghosts...could they be real?! Is YOUR house haunted? Have YOU ever seen a ghost? Quintus is home alone when things start to go bump in the night in this scary novella. It works well with any Roman House unit, and would be a quick read for anyone interested in Pliny's ghost story.

Syra sōla
(29 words)

Syra likes being alone, but there are too many people everywhere in Rome! Taking her friend's advice, Syra travels to the famous coastal towns of Pompeii and Herculaneum in search of solitude. Can she find it?

Syra et animālia
(35-85 words)

In this collection of 20 additional stories, Syra encounters animals around Rome. Use to provide more exposure to words from the novella, or as a Free Voluntary Reading (FVR) option for all students, independent from Syra sōla.

Poenica purpurāria
(16 cognates, 19 other words)

Poenica is an immigrant from Tyre, the Phoenician city known for its purple. She's an extraordinary purple-dyer who wants to become a tightrope walker! In this tale, her shop is visited by different Romans looking to get togas purpled, as well as an honored Vestal in need of a new trim on her sacred veil. Some requests are realistic—others ridiculous. Is life all work and no play? Can Poenica find the time to tightrope walk?

Olianna et sandalia extraōrdināria
(20 cognates, 20 other words)

Olianna learns more about herself and her family in this psychological thriller continuation of "Olianna et obiectum magicum." We begin at a critical moment in the original, yet in this new tale, not only does the magical object appear to Olianna, but so do a pair of extraordinary sandals! Olianna has some choices to make. How will her decisions affect the timeline? Will things ever get back to normal? If so, is that for the better, or worse?

Pīsō perturbātus
(36 words)

Piso minds his Ps and Qs..(and Cs...and Ns and Os) in this alliterative tongue-twisting tale touching upon the Roman concepts of ōtium and negōtium. Before Piso becomes a little poet, early signs of an old curmudgeon can be seen.

Drūsilla in Subūrā
(38 words)

Drusilla is a Roman girl who loves to eat, but doesn't know how precious her favorite foods are. In this tale featuring all kinds of Romans living within, and beyond their means, will Drusilla discover how fortunate she is?

Rūfus et arma ātra
(40 words)

Rufus is a Roman boy who excitedly awaits an upcoming fight featuring the best gladiator, Crixaflamma. After a victorious gladiatorial combat in the Flavian Amphitheater (i.e. Colosseum), Crixaflamma's weapons suddenly go missing! Can Rufus help find the missing weapons?

Rūfus et gladiātōrēs
(49-104 words)

This collection of 28 stories adds details to characters and events from Rūfus et arma ātra, as well as additional, new cultural information about Rome, and gladiators. Use to provide more exposure to words from the novella, or as a Free Voluntary Reading (FVR) option for all students, independent from Rūfus et arma ātra.

Level A
Beginner

Mārcus et scytala Caesaris
(20 cognates + 30 other words)

Marcus has lost something valuable containing a secret message that once belonged to Julius Caesar. Even worse, it was passed down to Marcus' father for safekeeping, and he doesn't know it's missing! As Marcus and his friend Soeris search Alexandria for clues of its whereabouts, hieroglyphs keep appearing magically. Yet, are they to help, or hinder? Can Marcus decipher the hieroglyphs with Soeris' help, and find Caesar's secret message?

71

Agrippīna aurīga

Agrippīna aurīga
(24 cognates + 33 other words)

Young Agrippina wants to race chariots, but a small girl from Lusitania couldn't possibly do that...could she?! After a victorious race in the stadium of Emerita, the local crowd favorite charioteer, Gaius Appuleius Dicloes, runs into trouble, and it's up to Agrippina to step into much bigger shoes. Can she take on the reins in this equine escapade?

diāria sīderum
(30-50 cognates + 30-50 other words)

Not much was known about The Architects—guardians of the stars—until their diaries were found in dark caves sometime in the Tenth Age. Explore their mysterious observations from the Seventh Age (after the Necessary Conflict), a time just before all evidence of their existence vanished for millenia! What happened to The Architects? Can you reconstruct the events that led to the disappearance of this ancient culture?

trēs amīcī
et mōnstrum saevum

trēs amīcī et mōnstrum saevum
(28 cognates + 59 other words)

What became of the quest that Quintus' mother entrusted to Sextus and Syra in Drūsilla et convīvium magārum? Quintus finds himself alone in a dark wood (or so he thinks). Divine intervention is needed to keep Quintus safe, but can the gods overcome an ancient evil spurred on by Juno's wrath? How can Quintus' friends help?

sitne amor?
(36 cognates, 53 other words)

Piso and Syra are friends, but is it more than that? Sextus and his non-binary friend, Valens, help Piso understand his new feelings, how to express them, and how NOT to express them! This is a story of desire, and discovery. Could it be love?

ecce, poēmata discipulīs
(77 cognates + 121 other words)

"Wait, we have to read...Eutropius...who's that?! Homework on a Friday?! Class for an hour straight without a break?! Oh no, more tests in Math?! What, no glossary?! Why can't we just read?! Honestly, I was in bed (but the teacher doesn't know!)..." This collection of 33 poems is a humorous yet honest reflection of school, Latin class, homework, tests, Romans, teaching, and remote learning.

Magister P's Poetry Practice

Ain't got rhythm? This book can help. You'll be presented with a rhythm and two words, phrases, or patterns, one of which matches. There are three levels, Noob, Confident, and Boss, with a total of 328 practice. This book draws its words, phrases, and patterns entirely from "ecce, poemata discipulis!," the book of poetry with over 270 lines of dactylic hexameter. Perhaps a first of its kind, too, this book can be used by students and their teacher at the same time. Therefore, consider this book a resource for going on a rhythmic journey together.

Agrippīna: māter fortis
(65 words)

Agrippīna is the mother of Rūfus and Pīsō. She wears dresses and prepares dinner like other Roman mothers, but she has a secret—she is strong, likes wearing armor, and can fight just like her husband! Can she keep this secret from her family and friends?

Līvia: māter ēloquens
(44-86 words)

Livia is the mother of Drusilla and Sextus. She wears dresses and prepares dinner like other Roman mothers, but she has a secret—she is well-spoken, likes wearing togas, and practices public speaking just like her brother, Gaius! Can she keep this secret from her family and friends? Livia: mater eloquens includes 3 versions under one cover. The first level, (Alpha), is simpler than Agrippina: mater fortis; the second level, (Beta) is the same level, and the third, (Gamma-Delta) is more complex.

Pīsō et Syra et pōtiōnēs mysticae
(163 cognates, 7 other words)

Piso can't seem to write any poetry. He's distracted, and can't sleep. What's going on?! Is he sick?! Is it anxiety?! On Syra's advice, Piso seeks mystical remedies that have very—different—effects. Can he persevere?

Drūsilla et convīvium magārum
(58 words)

Drusilla lives next to Piso. Like many Romans, she likes to eat, especially peacocks! As the Roman army returns, she awaits a big dinner party celebrating the return of her father, Julius. One day, however, she sees a suspicious figure give something to her brother. Who was it? Is her brother in danger? Is she in danger?

Level B
Advanced Beginner

mȳthos malus: convīvium Terregis
(41 cognates + 56 other words)

An obvious nod to Petronius' Cena Trimalchionis, yes, but this is not an adaptation, by any means. In this tale, Terrex can't get anything right during his latest dinner party. He's confused about Catullus' carmina, and says silly things left and right as his guests do all they can to be polite, though patience is running low. With guests even fact-checking amongst themselves, can Terrex say something remotely close to being true? Will the guests mind their manners and escape without offending their host?

sīgna zōdiaca Vol. 1
(63 cognates, 84 other words)
sīgna zōdiaca Vol. 2
(63 cognates, 92 other words)
sīgna zōdiaca Vol. 3
(62 cognates, 93 other words)

Do you like stories about gods and monsters? Did you know that the zodiac signs are based on Greek and Roman mythology? Your zodiac sign can tell you a lot about yourself, but not everyone feels that strong connection. Are your qualities different from your sign? Are they the same? Read signa zodiaca to find out! These readers are part non-fiction, and part Classical adaptation, providing information about the zodiac signs as well as two tiered versions of associated myths.

Level C
Low Intermediate

fragmenta Pīsōnis
(96 words)

This collection of poetry is inspired by scenes and characters from the Pisoverse, and features 50 new lines of poetry in dactylic hexameter, hendecasyllables, and scazon (i.e. limping iambics)! fragmenta Pīsōnis can be used as a transition to the Piso Ille Poetulus novella, or as additional reading for students comfortable with poetry having read the novella already.

Pīsō Ille Poētulus
(108 words)

Piso is a Roman boy who wants to be a great poet like Virgil. His family, however, wants him to be a soldier like his father. Can Piso convince his family that poetry is a worthwhile profession? Features 22 original, new lines of dactylic hexameter.

Pīsō: Tiered Versions
(68-138 words)

This novella combines features of Livia: mater eloquens with the tiered versions of the Piso Ille Poetulus story taken from its Teacher's Guide and Student Workbook. There are 4 different levels under one cover, which readers choose, switching between them at any time. Piso: Tiered Versions could be used as scaffolding for reading the original novella, Piso Ille Poetulus. Alternatively, it could be read independently as a Free Voluntary Reading (FVR) option, leaving it up to the learner which level to read.

Tiberius et Gallisēna ultima
(155 words)

Tiberius is on the run. Fleeing from an attacking Germanic tribe, the soldier finds himself separated from the Roman army. Trying to escape Gaul, he gets help from an unexpected source—a magical druid priestess (a "Gaul" in his language, "Celt" in hers). With her help, can Tiberius survive the punishing landscape of Gaul with the Germanic tribe in pursuit, and make his way home to see Rufus, Piso, and Agrippina once again?

...and more!
See magisterp.com for the latest:

teacher's materials
other books
audio

Made in the USA
Columbia, SC
06 September 2022

66194444R00048